Y 646 .72 Mey

Meyer, Carolyn.

Being beautiful :

MAY 30 1984
OCT 16 1995
JUL 2 2 2003
APR 7 2004
MAY 1 4 2005

Being Beautiful

By the Same Author

Coconut, the Tree of Life
Milk, Butter, and Cheese
Saw, Hammer, and Paint

with Jerome Wexler

Rock Tumbling, From Stones to Gems to Jewelry

Being Beautiful

THE STORY OF
COSMETICS FROM ANCIENT ART
TO MODERN SCIENCE
by Carolyn Meyer

ILLUSTRATED BY MARIKA

William Morrow and Company / New York 1977

Copyright © 1977 by Carolyn Meyer

All rights reserved. No part of this book may be reproduced or utilized in any form or by any means, electronic or mechanical, including photocopying, recording or by any information storage and retrieval system, without permission in writing from the Publisher. Inquiries should be addressed to William Morrow and Company, Inc., 105 Madison Ave., New York, N. Y. 10016.

Printed in the United States of America.

1 2 3 4 5 6 7 8 9 10

Library of Congress Cataloging in Publication Data

Meyer, Carolyn.
  Being beautiful.

  Bibliography: p. 93
  Includes index.
  SUMMARY: A survey of cosmetics and their use throughout history with a description of commercial manufacture, consumer advice, and recipes for homemade products.
  1. Beauty, Personal—Juvenile literature.
2. Cosmetics—Juvenile literature. [1. Beauty, Personal. 2. Cosmetics] I. Marika. II. Title.
RA778.M49   646.7′2   77-9935
ISBN 0-688-22125-4
ISBN 0-688-32125-9 lib. bdg.

CONTENTS

PART ONE. Down to Basics 7
Begin with the Skin 14
   Focus on the Face 18
      Cleaning Up / Masks / Moisturizers / Astringents / Milks, Creams, and Miracles
   Baths and Bodies 30
      Soap / Beauty Baths / Sweat and Odor / Perfumes / Golden Skin / Hands and Nails
Hair and Other Glories 47
   The Natural Crown 47
      Washing / Conditioning / Brushing / Curling and Straightening / Bleaching and Dyeing / Wigs
   Body Hair 58
   Teeth 60
   Eyes 61

PART TWO. Making Up 63
Pioneering Women 68
Painting in the Twentieth Century 71
   What's in Those Jars? 76

"Hope is what we sell . . ." 78
Danger! Beautifiers! 81
  Allergies
Last Resort: Surgery 86
Men Painting 89
Looking Ahead 91

Bibliography 93
Index 94

PART ONE
Down to Basics

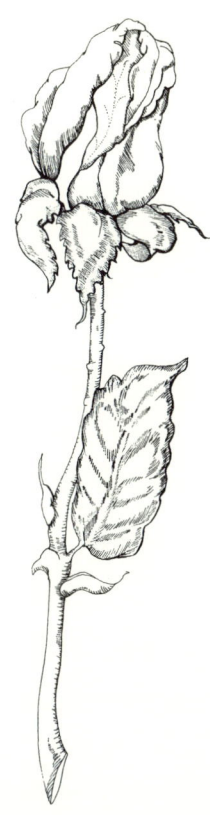

Take a look in the mirror. How do you feel about what you see? Probably you are only partly satisfied with your appearance. You think you would be more attractive, closer to being beautiful, if only you had more of this or less of that or a different color or shape of something else. It might surprise you to know that practically everybody feels the same way about themselves, even people who are considered beautiful by practically everybody else. One of the largest industries in the United States is based on the idea of helping all these dissatisfied people move closer to their idea of being beautiful.

People have been concerned with beauty—their own and others'—for as far back as history can see. Philosophers have tried to define beauty; poets have attempted to describe it; men have admired it and worshiped it; women have worked hard to acquire it and preserve it. Beauty in an individual has always been recognized and praised, but nobody has ever been able to say, for all time and for all people, what beauty *is*.

Beauty is an idea that constantly changes as people

change the ways in which they live. For instance, when most ordinary women worked long hours under a hot sun, tanned skin was considered unattractive. Being beautiful required pale, fragile-looking skin—the kind you could have only if you were rich enough to pay someone else to do the hard outside labor for you. Today most ordinary women work inside kitchens or offices, and only those with money to spend on vacations in sunny places or time to visit a health club can afford suntanned skin. So now a tan has become desirable, despite the dire warnings of doctors and other skin-care experts. It's beautiful because it's an indication of status, although most people are not aware of this reason.

Fat *vs.* thin is another changing standard of beauty, and again it has to do with money and status. When people had to toil for their food and only the wealthy had plenty to eat, plumpness was considered beautiful. Think of all those paintings you've seen in museums of well-padded nudes. Today, though, with food so abundant in the United States that overeating is common and obesity a health problem, fat is "out," and people spend a great deal of money trying to get rid of it.

Some cases of changing standards of beauty are rather easily explained, such as the shift from plump and pale to lean and tan, but not all are so obvious. Consider, for example, the treatment of eyebrows. Sometimes they have been shaved off or plucked out completely and replaced with frankly artificial paint or even bits of mouse skin applied in a more attractive position, wherever that might have been. While some women have painted on thick brows or plucked them to a nearly invisible line, most have wanted a wide space between them. But not in some Oriental cultures, where eyebrows that grow together across the bridge of the nose have been much admired.

Every new age produces its own concept of what is beautiful, influenced by a handful of pacesetters: inventive, individualistic women with their own personal idea of beauty. Gradually more and more people copy and imitate these ideas until they are so common that they are not novel or startling anymore. Your grandmother may have been influenced by the style of theatrical actresses in her day. Your mother probably found her ideal at the movies. Perhaps your own concept of beauty is derived from popular television stars. Certainly, too, you are impressed by fashion models in the magazines you read, not only by how they dress (fashion is another, closely related story) but by the way they fix their hair and make up their faces. And the beauty columnists in these magazines, working closely with manufacturers of cosmetics, help to shape the picture of ideal beauty in your mind. No matter what that picture is, your self-image—the way you see yourself, the way you think you look—probably doesn't come even close to it.

The fact is that almost no one's self-image is at all accurate. Studies show that the mirror *does* lie to the woman studying her own reflection. Few women are able to decide whether their faces are round or oval or square. They are even less able to describe their bodies accurately. After fat people lose a great deal of weight and are indeed quite thin, they still see themselves as fat. This is also true of thin people who gain weight; they imagine themselves always as thin, no matter what the scales indicate.

Dissatisfaction with one's looks is felt much more strongly by some people, who will try everything possible to change their looks. This dissatisfaction seldom has much to do with the way the person *really* looks. The objective truth is unimportant. What really matters is what you think of yourself. If you believe you are good looking, then you will *act* as though you are, and—strange as it may seem—people will *react* to you as though you are, and their reactions, completing the cycle, will make you *believe* you are. In his first book, *Childhood,* part of the autobiography begun when he was twenty-four, Russian author Leo Tolstoy wrote, "I am convinced that nothing has so marked an influence on the direction of a man's mind as his appearance, and not his appearance so much as his conviction that it is attractive or unattractive." Young girls who have gotten into enough trouble to be sent to correctional institutions almost always have a very low opinion of their own looks, even when they are, by the standards of others, quite pretty. Feeling that they are ugly is apparently one reason they behave that way.

Perhaps the most important element in beauty is not a perfectly-shaped nose or unblemished skin, but self-confidence. If you believe in your own beauty, you will be beautiful. But if you don't believe, nothing—not complicated surgery or a fortune spent on cosmetics—can make you beautiful.

But what's the point of being beautiful, of striving for the impossible ideal? The most obvious answer is to be

"attractive" in the literal sense: to attract the admiration of other people, particularly the opposite sex. People who feel attractive also feel accepted, which brings us right back to self-confidence again.

The need to be attractive fuels the gigantic American beauty business: the cosmetics industry, the advertising industry that services its largest client, and related businesses, such as beauty salons. Although the cosmetics industry did not actually get started until the twentieth century and has become the giant that it is only in the past few decades, men and women—but mostly women—have used cosmetics as long as history has been recorded.

Cosmetics comes from the Greek word *kosmetikos*, "skilled in arranging," which gets its origin from *kosmos*, "order." The Food, Drug, and Cosmetic Act of 1938 defines cosmetics as "articles intended to be rubbed, poured, sprinkled, or sprayed on, introduced into, or otherwise applied to the human body or any part thereof for cleansing, beautifying, promoting attractiveness, or altering the appearance." The history of cosmetics is as old as the desire to be beautiful, and it tells us a great deal about who and what we are today.

BEGIN WITH THE SKIN

For thousands of years people have searched for ways to preserve the appearance of youth (and youth is one way of defining beauty, when you are older) by putting things on their skin. Some of these skin treatments are simple, have been in use for centuries, and are still in use today. Some are museum pieces, interesting to read about, but you'd never want to try them. Others are products that have been concocted by cosmetics manufacturers, fancily packaged, heavily advertised with miraculous claims, and sold at very high prices; often you can achieve the same results using inexpensive items from the drugstore or supermarket.

Once you understand how the skin works and what it

needs to keep it in good order, you can take care of your skin with very little money. Some people enjoy performing a regular beauty ritual; it makes them feel as though they are doing something good for themselves. Others want to do whatever is necessary as quickly and efficiently as possible. The results will be about the same.

From a purely practical point of view, the skin is a marvelous organ, protecting the body from the environment outside and maintaining an even temperature inside. It weighs close to seven pounds and covers an area of about nineteen square feet. The skin is surprisingly complex tissue, made up of two main layers. The inner layer, the dermis, contains blood vessels, nerve endings, sweat glands, sebaceous glands that produce an oil (sebum) to keep the skin soft and moist, follicles from which hair grows, and muscles. The outer layer, the epidermis, is much thinner. New cells constantly multiply along its inner side, pushing the older cells to the surface where they flatten out and overlap like shingles on a roof. These cells are continually being shed and replaced by new ones.

One requirement for healthy skin is that the dead, dirty skin cells be removed regularly and that the right amount of sebum be maintained in that outer layer. Too much sebum: oily skin that sometimes breaks out in pimples. Too little sebum: dry skin that wrinkles and ages quickly. The amount of sebum varies with the individual, determined by age, heredity, and general health. A big part of the cosmetics industry is based on products that attempt to regulate the amount of oil in the skin.

The human being is the only animal that shows its physical age, and one way age shows is through changes that take place in the skin. Before you were born, while you were still in the womb, your skin existed under perfect conditions of temperature and moisture. But as soon as you entered the world, the problems began. At birth your skin is very thin, dry, and delicate. You are prone to rashes, prickly heat in summer, chapping in cold winter weather. As you get older, your skin becomes tougher, but it also begins to lose its perfect smoothness.

Then with the onset of adolescence and changing hormones, other problems begin to develop. The skin may produce more sebum than it needs. The pores—ducts leading from the sweat glands to the surface—become clogged with hardened oils, and whiteheads form under the skin. Surface dirt collects in the pores, causing blackheads, and infections develop in the sebaceous glands. Bad pimples, from acute infections in the tissues under the epidermis, may leave scars when they clear up.

Eventually, however, all that hormonal activity calms down. Still, the skin may be oily and require extra cleansing, or it may be too dry and easily irritated. Dry skin develops wrinkles earlier than oily skin. Some skin combines both qualities: oily nose and chin, dry forehead; oily back, dry arms and legs. And some people are lucky enough to have normal skin, with just the right amount of oil where it is needed.

As you grow older, your skin will become drier and small lines will start to form, beginning with the face where the skin is most fragile. As the pads of fat beneath the skin gradually melt away with age, deep creases and wrinkles form around the mouth and across the forehead. This process is an inevitable part of growing older, and it happens to everyone. But despite the fact that every living person eventually shows the signs of aging, no one wants to look old. People—and especially women—try to stay young-looking (and therefore more beautiful) for as long as they can. How fast your skin ages depends partly on your heredity and partly on how you take care of your skin when you are still young and believe that old age is something that happens to other people.

Proper care of this tough-but-delicate, nineteen-square-foot body covering begins with general health: enough

sleep, fresh air, exercise, and the right kind of diet. Vitamin A, the skin vitamin, is found in yellow foods that are rich in carotene: eggs, cheese, carrots, apricots, cantaloupes. (Don't overdo the amount, though; too much carotene can turn your skin temporarily yellow, and massive doses of the vitamin, taken in tablet form, cause some people's hair to fall out.) You also need plenty of fish, liver, whole milk, and leafy, dark-green vegetables. What you don't need, of course, are sweets, chocolates, and too many animal fats.

Focus on the Face

Beauty is like a religion; for some people it *is* a religion. There are many schools of belief and hundreds of experts dispensing the gospel, many claims to the real truth, and endless contradictions. All seem convincing—until you run up against another theory that's even more convincing. Perhaps the best procedure is to try out the different beliefs, and after you've given them a fair test, decide which one works best for you.

Cleaning Up

Take such a simple act as washing your face. The skin is constantly shedding dead cells, and the air is full of pollutants landing on your epidermis and sticking in your pores. Your face is dirty and you want to get it clean. If you have oily skin, you want to get rid of the excess grease. If you have dry skin, you want to lubricate it. Immediately the controversy erupts.

Some say that soap and water are best for your face. Others claim that the only thing fit to use is a cleansing cream. The cream advocates always propose a test: wash your face first with soap and water, and when you think you've got it clean, apply cleansing cream and tissue it off. See all that dirt you missed with ordinary soap and water? The soapers retort: cream just smears the dirt around; it doesn't remove it. But soap is drying, cry the creamers. Nonsense, respond the soapers, not if you rinse it all off. And then someone chimes in: think of all those germs that breed in a washcloth!

Some people don't use soap *or* cream to clean their faces. If you'd rather not pick sides, try this old-fashioned recipe:

OATMEAL SCRUBBER   Put a handful of plain, uncooked oatmeal in the foot of a nylon stocking. Tie it shut and cut off the rest of the stocking. Wet the scrubber and gently wash your face with it. Rinse your face thoroughly. Replace with fresh oatmeal every couple of days.

If you decide to use soap, try to find the mildest one you can. Don't bother with medicated soaps or cleansers, which can't do much good in the short time in which they are in contact with the skin, or with "superfatted" soaps, which also must be completely rinsed away and merely cost more. The skin is slightly acid, one way it protects itself against bacteria. Soap is usually alkaline. Although healthy skin returns to its natural acidity by itself, make sure all traces of soap are rinsed away. For generations, women have used diluted lemon juice or vinegar to help restore the protective "acid mantle" of the skin.

COSMETIC VINEGAR   Mix equal parts white or cider vinegar with plain water, and pat it on your clean face with gauze or cotton balls.

The use of hot or cold water on the face is also the subject of debate. Some women steam their faces over a pan of boiling water or soak them with hot washcloths to dissolve the sebum that may be blocking the pores and to improve circulation. Other experts disapprove of these habits, warning that steam and hot water are hard on the skin and that the rosy glow isn't good circulation at all but simple irritation. Some people always end a face cleansing with a splash of cold water, because it feels invigorating. But cold water doesn't "close the pores" as it was once thought, and the extremes in temperature may be too harsh. For those who prefer a middle path, wash with lukewarm water and rinse with warm or cool water.

Masks

Since earliest times, women have strived to improve their complexions with beauty masks, probably the oldest facial treatment known. Recipes for such masks could fill a book. Most of them are for cleaning the skin and removing dead cells, beyond what plain soap-and-water washing or creaming can accomplish. Some, used by older women worried about wrinkles, are for "tightening the skin."

Masks don't really shrink the pores or remove wrinkles, but they do remove dirt and they do feel good—especially when you take them off. They put tension on the skin as they dry, causing the tiny blood vessels to swell a little. That's why, when you rinse off the mask, you'll look pink-cheeked and healthy—temporarily. Use them only about once a week.

EGG-WHITE MASK   Separate an egg, store the yolk for another use, and pat the white on your face with cotton. Let it dry for about fifteen minutes and then rinse it off.

FULLER'S-EARTH MASK   Sold inexpensively at drugstores, fuller's earth is a variety of kaolin, a kind of clay. It is good for soaking up excess oil and impurities from

the skin. Put a spoonful in the palm of your hand, and mix it with liquid—plain water, or a little lemon juice, pineapple juice, cucumber juice, or egg white—just enough to make a paste. Smear it on your face, leaving goggle-sized openings around your eyes. Leave it on for about fifteen or twenty minutes. It will dry hard, like cement; you won't be able to smile without your face cracking. When the time is up, rinse off the mask with plenty of water. Feel good?

Moisturizers

Cleaning the skin is not enough. It must also be protected—from sunburn, wind, chapping, drying out in artificially heated and air-conditioned rooms, from pollutants in the air. Moisturizers are the best protection. From earliest times, women have tried everything imaginable (and some things unimaginable) to keep their skin soft.

Contrary to the claims of cosmetics manufacturers and advertisers, dermatologists and others professionally concerned with care of the human skin say you can't put moisture back into the skin with a moisturizer. All you can do is coat the skin with a thin film of oil that will prevent further evaporation of water from the tissue in addition to keeping the skin smooth and supple. (Some even say it's the *water* in the moisturizer that is the most helpful ingredient, which appears to contradict the idea that moisture can't be put back into the skin.)

A moisturizer is technically called an "emollient," a substance that softens and soothes the skin. The range of possibilities is enormous; just about any oily substance has at one time or another found favor as an emollient. And, not unexpectedly, there is considerable controversy about which oils are the best emollients. Here are some common ones.

LARD Plain white fat from a pig's belly, sold in grocery stores for pastry making and other cookery, it is easily absorbed by the skin and is an ingredient in many cosmetic creams. Use it straight.

LANOLIN Obtained from the oil glands of sheep, it absorbs and holds water to the skin. Because it often causes allergies and is sticky and rather messy to apply, lanolin is not often used plain, but it is a highly favored ingredient in cosmetics.

MINERAL OIL   It stays on the surface of the skin, leaving a protective coating, but many people don't like the shiny look. Some experts claim that mineral oil, like petroleum jelly (Vaseline), another cheap and efficient emollient, actually dries the skin. Others swear by them.

VEGETABLE OILS   Any oil from the grocer's shelf can be used just as it comes from the bottle.

GLYCERIN   A by-product of soap making, glycerin has been used as a moisturizer for generations. Glycerin is a "humectant," meaning that it attracts moisture from the air. This makes it an important ingredient in modern cosmetics, not only because it's good for your skin, but because it helps keep cosmetics—face creams, etc.—from drying out in the jar. Some people contend that if glycerin can draw moisture from the air, it can also draw moisture from your skin, especially in very dry weather. There have also been complaints that it irritates the skin of some users, making it rough and red.

Despite what advertisers and beauty writers want you to believe, skin cannot be fed from the outside. You can dab all kinds of skin "food" on your face, but they will not nourish it, although they may act as an emollient or moisturizer. The *only* way to nourish your skin is to eat the proper foods.

Nevertheless, people have attempted to feed their skin externally for years and years. Here are some of their suggestions, which you can try out yourself. They can't hurt you, and they will help to keep your skin soft and soothed.

CUCUMBER   One of the oldest moisturizers known,

dating from the days of Cleopatra, cucumber is an ingredient in many modern creams and lotions. The easiest way to use it is to keep a fresh one in the refrigerator and simply rub the cut end all over your face. Or you can slice it or mash it and spread the pulp on your face while you lie down and rest for a few minutes.

STRAWBERRIES Mash a few, and spread the juice and pulp on your face. Strawberry juice is also widely used in the so-called natural cosmetics. If strawberries are out of season, or you'd rather eat them than wear them (if you're allergic to them, don't do either one), you can try a variety of other fresh, slightly acid fruits that are supposedly good for your skin, such as white grapes or watermelon.

AVOCADO   Mash this very oily fruit, and spread the pulp on your face. When you wipe it off with a tissue, leave some of the oily film.

BANANA   Use the same as avocado.

TOMATO   Lay thin slices on your face and rub in the pulp gently. It definitely helps to restore the acid mantle and may also be good for skin problems.

MAYONNAISE   Use it right from the jar or make your own. It contains oil, egg yolk, and lemon juice, all supposedly good skin foods.

OATMEAL   Put a tablespoon in a cup, and add enough warm water to make a thin paste. Spread it on your face, and leave it until it dries; then wash it off with warm water.

HONEY   Mix 1 tablespoon of warm honey with 1 teaspoon of lemon juice or pineapple juice. Spread it on your face, and leave it for a half hour; then rinse it off. Or try mixing equal parts of honey and mashed raw apple, or honey and raw wheat germ. Pat the mixture on, leave it on for a while, and wash it off.

Astringents

Known in the cosmetics industry by a variety of names —fresheners, toners, pore lotions, skin tonics—astringents are used to remove some of the excess oil and to "shrink" the pores that make skin look coarse. According to some doctors, an astringent doesn't actually reduce the size of the pores, but it does irritate them, causing them

to puff up a little and look smaller. Some astringents expand the small blood vessels, giving the skin a rosy, healthy-looking glow. Evaporation cools and refreshes the skin. Rather than buying the claims and packaging of advertised cosmetics, you can mix your own astringent, using simple ingredients that women have thought for centuries made their skin less greasy and smoother.

BUTTERMILK Marie Antoinette used it on both her face and her bosom, as did generations of women before her. Pat it on and then rinse it off with water. Yogurt or sour cream are good substitutes; it's the acid in all of them that produces the astringent effect.

WITCH HAZEL   Obtained from a small, shrubby plant, witch hazel contains tannic acid. Splash it on right from the bottle, or mix it with a little pineapple juice, which contains an enzyme thought to be good for the skin.

ALCOHOL   Use it plain, wiping your skin with cotton balls soaked in it. Alcohol is the main ingredient of most commercial astringents, but too much of it can stimulate the sebaceous glands to secrete even more oil.

Milks, Creams, and Miracles

Milk has always enjoyed a reputation for being good for your skin. You can, of course, drink it—it's rich in Vitamin A. You can also wash with it; some women used to fill their bathtubs with it. If your skin is dry, try washing it with cream; if it's oily, use skim milk or one of the cultured milks, such as buttermilk or yogurt. Be sure to rinse it all off with fresh water to prevent the development of bacteria.

Because milk is regarded highly, many modern cosmetic preparations are called "milks," even though most contain no milk, or only a trace. They are diluted cleansing creams, emulsions of tiny droplets of mineral oil and water that do indeed look milky.

Cleansing creams, or cold creams, have been around since the early days of Greece and Rome when a physician named Galen stirred up a mixture of olive oil, beeswax, water, and rose petals, the forerunner of all face creams.

They're called cold creams because when the oil-water emulsion breaks down, the water evaporates, leaving the skin feeling cool.

With predictable regularity, the cosmetics industry announces the discovery of a fantastic new product that will do what no cream has ever done before: remove wrinkles, prevent them, delay them, or hide them. To women who are afraid of getting older and losing their youthful looks, the promises of the advertisers seem to offer exactly what they need. There have been times in the past few decades when women have willingly paid huge prices for creams containing mink oil, turtle oil, or jelly obtained from the queen bee. Many of such "precious ingredients" are waste products from other industries, obtained cheaply by the cosmetics companies, fancily packaged, heavily advertised, and sold at high prices. Thousands of women have eagerly spent fifteen dollars for an ounce of cream that cost only a few cents to manufacture, perhaps believing that "if it's this expensive, it has to be good."

As emollients, mink oil, turtle oil, and royal jelly were as good as any other—but no better. Hormone creams, another highly touted miracle, were in fact able to penetrate the skin and actually did appear to retard the aging process. But the price in this case *was* too high; the hormones that were beneficial to the skin were possible causes of cancer in other organs. There simply are no miracles in cosmetics, although it seems to be part of human nature to hope for one.

Sometimes, no matter how well you care for your skin, a pimple, blotch, or cold sore can put in an unsightly appearance. Vitamin E has been publicized as a cure-all when applied in an oil base directly to the problem. But many experts say the vitamin has no value used this way. A better choice is cod-liver oil, rich in Vitamins A and D, either plain or as the main ingredient in a healing ointment.

Baths and Bodies

Bathing—in speedy shower or leisurely tub—is so much a part of our daily lives that it's hard to believe it has been in and out of fashion numerous times in the course of history. The ancient Persians looked down on bathing as unfitting for males, but in Egypt people of both sexes bathed regularly as part of a sacred ritual. The Greeks also bathed, believing that cleanliness was essential to beauty. When the Romans took baths, it was a leisure pursuit, chiefly of the men, a relaxing luxury as well as a social occasion.

But the decline and fall of Rome also meant the decline of bathing, and for centuries few people throughout Europe ever climbed into a tub. Perhaps because luxurious baths had been associated with the decadence of Rome, churchmen in the Middle Ages preached that bathing was sinful and went so far as to claim that a dirty body was the sign of a clean soul. In later years Crusaders returning from the Middle East brought word of lavish bathing in that part of the world. But Europe was a cold place; the castles were drafty and chilly. Heating and carrying enough water for a proper bath made it a luxury seldom indulged in. Eventually, maybe because it *was* such a luxury, bathing came into style among the upper classes.

Soap

No one knows where or how soap was first invented. The Greeks didn't use it; they oiled their bodies and scraped off the dirt and dead skin with special tools. But someone, at some indefinite time, by some unrecorded accident, discovered that water mixed with wood ashes and then combined with animal fats produced a substance that seemed to take the dirt off their skin more easily than plain water did. Some historians think the Romans learned soapmaking from the ancient tribes they conquered; the Roman naturalist and encyclopedist, Pliny the Elder, described the soap used by Germanic tribes. Others believe the Romans themselves were probably the first makers of soap.

In any case, the Spanish became the leading soap makers. Castile, a fine white soap, takes its name from the district where high-grade olive trees yielded oil used in producing the best soap of the day. Next the French took over the leadership, from the ninth century to the thirteenth, when they yielded supremacy to the Italians. About this time the English, too, began manufacturing soap. The whaling ships supplied the oil. Business prospered, but for many years there was such a high tax on soap in England that most poor people couldn't afford it.

In the American colonies, housewives made their own soap. First they prepared the lye, a strong alkali still basic to modern soapmaking, by dripping water through wood ashes. They mixed the lye with fat saved from cooking meat, and the big open kettle was set over a fire to boil. The lye reacted chemically with the grease and produced soap—harsh and bad-smelling, but it was all they had. Then modern chemistry took over and improved the ingredients, and by 1850 soapmaking was a fast-growing and highly competitive industry in the United States. Advertising was introduced, and photographs and statements of famous and beautiful women reminded ordinary women that soap was essential to a good complexion. It was through selling soap that the American advertising industry got its start and made its mark. The advertising worked, too; the United States became the number one user of soap.

In the 1930's, synthetic detergents began to replace soap in a number of uses. While soap is the result of the chemical reaction between alkali and fat, synthetic detergents are compounded from a variety of raw materials. Not only do synthetic detergents clean as efficiently as soap, they don't react with the minerals in hard water to form a scum that leaves a ring in the bathtub or a dull film on hair. But they do have their drawbacks, too. Ecologists claim they are responsible for destroying the balance of life in lakes and streams. And some beauty experts say the ingredients are drying to skin and hair, although detergents are less alkaline than most bar soaps.

All detergents—soap is one too—act in about the same way. First they lower the surface tension of the water, the tension that gives drops of water their shape and keeps a barely overfilled glass from running over. Then they break up the oily film that traps the particles of dirt, letting them float away.

A few soaps and many detergents advertise that they are neutral, or have a pH value of 7. The "pH" stands for "potential of hydrogen"; pH 7 is neutral—like pure water —neither acid nor alkaline. Skin, which is slightly acid, normally has a pH from 5.5 to 6.5. Most soaps have a pH higher than 7.

There are also some so-called natural detergents, obtained from plants containing saponin, a nongreasy, nonalkaline substance that foams when the leaves are bruised. The roots of the yucca plant, the fruit of the soapberry tree in South America, a lilylike plant called the soap apple, the soapbark tree in the Andes, and bouncing Bet, a kind of wild pink abundant in North America, also known as soapwort—all contain saponin, used for washing by primitive peoples and included in many sophisticated cosmetic formulations.

Beauty Baths

Off and on, since the days of the Romans, there has been the appreciation of the bath as a means not only of cleaning the skin but beautifying it and refreshing the spirit as well. It wasn't always necessary to have water available; there were famous beauties in history who supposedly soaked in a tub full of crushed strawberries or of asses' milk. Bathing in milk—cows' will do when asses' milk is scarce—has long been associated with beautiful skin. Mary, Queen of Scots, started the fad of washing in wine. This may not have been so wasteful as it sounds; the mistress of Czar Alexander I dipped each morning in a tank of Spanish wine, which was then bottled and sold to the czar's appreciative subjects.

If it's not convenient to fill your tub with such luxurious materials, there are many other ways to give your body a treat. Colored and perfumed bath salts are little more than ordinary table salt with borax added to soften the water. Bubble baths contain borax, which means there will be lots of foamy bubbles and no scum to clean out of the tub afterwards. But many people have been found sensitive to bath salts, especially if they're not completely dissolved or if too strong a concentration is used.

Here are some harmless, beneficial, inexpensive baths that you can formulate yourself. Remember that bath water should be comfortably warm but not too hot. Very hot water is as hard on the rest of your body as it is on your face.

SALT   A cup of ordinary table salt added to bath water feels good and makes the skin silky to the touch. While you're in the tub, scour your elbows, knees, and feet with a handful of wet salt to remove dead cells and soften the skin. However, you will not get much lather from your soap in salt water, and the salty residue that's left on your skin may be drying.

CUCUMBER AND GLYCERIN   Peel, chop, and mash a cucumber, strain out the pulp, and mix the liquid with an equal amount of glycerin. Add a couple of spoonfuls of the mixture to your bath water. Keep the rest tightly covered and labeled in the refrigerator.

OATMEAL   Pour about a cup of raw oatmeal in a cotton sock or in the foot of a nylon stocking, and tie it up tight so it doesn't clog the drain. Toss this in the bath while the water runs to release the oil in the oatmeal, and then use it to give yourself a rubdown. It makes the skin feel smooth and satiny.

HERB-AND-FLOWER BATH If the main point of the bath is to surround yourself in sweet smells, put an assortment of dried flower petals, herbs like sweet basil or rosemary, or a handful of pine needles in the foot of a nylon stocking, tie it under the tap so the water runs through it as the tub fills, or toss it in a tub of very hot water to steep like a tea bag as the water cools.

BAKING-SODA BATH   If your skin is dry or irritated, a half cup or more of baking soda added to the bath water will relieve the irritation.

Sweat and Odor

Of all our reasons for bathing, perhaps the most important is to wash away odor-causing perspiration. There are over two million sweat glands in the dermis, the inner layer of the skin. Most of them are eccrine glands that regulate the temperature of the body and help to keep the skin soft by secreting sweat, a colorless fluid, mostly water, that evaporates so quickly you are not aware of it, except in hot weather or during exercise. Some parts of the body, such as the head, neck, and back, sweat more than others. The hands and feet don't perspire more as body temperature rises but as a response to fear or nervousness. One theory is that the hands of prehistoric man sweated so that he could get a better grip on tree limbs when he was escaping from danger.

Certain areas of the body, such as the armpits and around the sex organs, have a second type of sweat gland, the apocrine, that produces a more complex substance than ordinary sweat, rich in organic material. In fact, the armpits do not perspire as much as you may think, but because evaporation is more difficult, sweat accumulates there. Both types of sweat are odorless until bacteria begins to act on them. Sweat from the apocrines has a far more pungent odor than perspiration from the eccrines and was once an important part of sexual attraction.

Not anymore. In our culture we regard the odor of sweat as unpleasant. Not everyone does, even in Western cultures, and not everyone in our own always has. Regular bathing is the easiest way to get rid of sweat before an odor develops, but in centuries past few people could or would bathe often. The wealthy masked the smell of their unwashed bodies and unwashed clothes with liberal dousings of perfume; people who couldn't afford the expensive perfumes simply accepted their own odors. But as time went on, many people, particularly in the United States, became rather obsessive about smells; they set out not merely to mask odors but to eliminate them entirely. Deodorants were invented to stop or slow down the growth of bacteria that cause sweat to have the characteristic smell we consider undesirable. Antiperspirants were developed to prevent the flow of sweat in certain areas, usually the underarms. There are no simple alternatives to the chemical formulas of deodorants and antiperspirants, but there are a couple of inexpensive stopgaps, in addition to frequent bathing.

WITCH HAZEL   A dash of this mild antiseptic under each arm will help to retard the development of odor.

CORNSTARCH   Although it will not eliminate odor, a dusting of cornstarch absorbs sweat and makes you feel drier. Most commercial body powders are made with talc, a soft mineral that allows the powder to glide over the skin more easily. Cornstarch doesn't have this silky feeling, but it is inexpensive. Use it as it comes from the box or keep it in a jar with a shaker top.

For a more luxurious body powder, try scenting the cornstarch with flowers. Mix two teaspoons of orrisroot (purchased from the drugstore) with a one-pound box of cornstarch in a large casserole with a lid. Cover the powders with a layer of cheesecloth or a handkerchief and pile fresh flower petals on top of it. Every day remove the wilted flowers and put in fresh ones. Do this for a few weeks. Eventually the scent of the flowers will permeate the powders. When you're satisfied with the scent, pour the powders into containers with tight lids.

Orrisroot has a mild fragrance of its own and is often used by the perfume industry to fix other scents, to keep them from fading. You can also make the powder without the orrisroot, but the scent will not linger.

Perfumes

Not smelling bad is not enough for most people; they also want to smell *good*. The perfume industry is a very old one, nearly as old as cosmetics, and it has always involved a great deal of secrecy. The word *perfume* means "through smoke," and the first perfumes were incense. Later people dried flowers, leaves, and spices, and they powdered them to use in religious festivals and to make themselves smell good. Egyptian women prepared balls of perfumed fats, which they tucked in their hair; body heat melted the fat and slowly released the fragrance.

Eventually perfumes and their production became increasingly complicated and sophisticated. There are a number of different techniques for obtaining perfumes. Generally speaking, an oil is prepared that contains the essence of the flowers or other source of the desired fragrance. This essential oil is then diluted with alcohol. High concentrations of oils are used in the most expensive perfumes, and only tiny dabs are applied to the pulse points so that the heat of the body releases the scent. Colognes, invented by an Italian barber who settled in the German city of Cologne, generally contain much more alcohol and can be splashed on more generously; the alcohol evaporates quickly and leaves behind a subtle scent. Perfume is more expensive than cologne but the fragrance lasts longer.

If you want to try making your own perfume, you need

time, patience, and a continuing and ample supply of fresh flowers or herbs. The methods are basically simple.

INFUSION This is a little like making tea. Gather enough fresh flower petals or herbs to fill a glass jar loosely, add water to cover, close the jar tightly, and put it in a warm place. Every three days pour the mixture through two layers of cheesecloth to remove the old flowers, and add fresh petals to the liquid. Do this for several weeks. The result will be quite mild.

MACERATION This is similar in technique to infusion, but instead of using water, cover the flower petals or herbs with mineral oil, about 2 cups of oil to ½ cup of tightly packed flower petals. Warm the oil slightly, and keep the jar in the sun or some other warm place. Keep the lid on tight. Every day strain the mixture through cheesecloth and add fresh flowers. Do this daily for at least a month. Obviously this project is best attempted in summer when the supply of flowers is limitless. You can start with lilacs, go on to lily of the valley and roses when the lilacs fade, and so on through the blooming season.

ENFLEURAGE Because this technique requires the use of pure alcohol, you may not be able to manage it. In some states pure alcohol cannot be obtained at all; in others it can be purchased from a liquor store or from a drugstore with a prescription. (Rubbing alcohol has a strong smell of its own.) You can substitute vodka, with an adult's permission and assistance in obtaining it, of course. Make sure, however, the vodka is really scentless. First, coat the bottom of a large glass baking dish with a thin layer of lard. Then gather a couple of handfuls of fresh flower petals, and sprinkle them over the lard. Cover the baking dish tightly with a lid or with a layer of aluminum foil, sealing the edges with tape. Keep it in a dark place overnight. The next day pick out any wilted flower petals and replace them with fresh ones. Seal them in. Do this every day for at least two or three weeks. Then remove all the remaining petals, and set the baking dish in a pan of hot water to melt the lard. Pour the melted fat into a jar, straining it through two layers of cheesecloth to remove any bits of flowers. Add an equal amount of alcohol or vodka and seal with a tight-fitting lid. Store the jar in a dark place for another two or three weeks—the longer the better. In the first stage, the flowers transfer their scent to the fat; during the second the fat transfers the scent to the alcohol. When at last the alcohol has picked up most of the scent, pour it off into pretty little perfume bottles with tight stoppers. The lard that remains is called pomade; pack it in jars, and use it as a moisturizer.

Enfleurage is the method used commercially for producing only the finest and most expensive perfumes, but the method is then carried one step further: the alcohol is removed by distillation, leaving behind a minute quantity of flower-scented essential oil, called the "absolute," from which the perfume is then compounded. Sometimes there are as many as two hundred ingredients in a fine perfume, and the formula is a closely guarded secret.

If this process seems too time-consuming and painstaking, you can purchase many essential oils from a druggist or craft-supply shop. Ordinary scents, like lavender and orange, are usually readily available; the more exotic —ylang-ylang, for instance—may have to be specially ordered. You'll find recipes for combining these oils in books about perfumery, or you can experiment with your own.

Golden Skin

Not many years ago, fine ladies sat in the shade or strolled under parasols or hid beneath big hats and long sleeves and skirts, if indeed they ventured out at all. Today women seek the sun and expose as much of their skin to it as possible and legal. Suntan is in fashion; sunburn, however, is not. Not everyone realizes that a tan is actually a slight burn and may be harmful.

Melanin, the pigmentation in the skin (as well as in the hair and eyes), is the body's protection against the dangerous ultraviolet rays of the sun. Dark-skinned people have more melanin than fair-skinned and so are better protected against ultraviolet light, but even the darkest skin can become sunburned. Freckles are collections of melanin near the surface of the skin, often caused by sunlight. People used to consider freckles an abomination and tried to get rid of them by bleaching them with lemon juice; today a sprinkling is considered attractive, and false freckles, like fake sunburn, are not unheard of.

Doctors have been warning us of the dangers of sunburn for some time. Although the sun is a source of Vitamin D, they say it's probably better to get it from vitamin-rich foods than from a potentially dangerous source. Constant tanning often dries out skin and, therefore, makes it more prone to wrinkling and premature aging. Some doctors even claim that too much sunburn can lead to cancer.

But since most people ignore such doomsaying and go ahead and lie in the sun anyway, because it feels good and everyone thinks a tan looks good, the best solution is to take sensible precautions against burning. One is to limit the time of exposure—no more than ten or fifteen minutes a day on each side. The other is to use an effective sunscreen to protect the skin from ultraviolet rays and an emollient to prevent drying.

Although many inexpensive preparations promote tanning and keep the skin soft and moisturized, most do not contain a protective sunscreen. Nearly any oil from the grocer's shelf can be used as a suntan oil, but only sesame-seed oil has slight screening properties. And these oils seem too messy for most people, who dislike the greasy feeling. The best idea is to buy a good commercial sunscreen preparation and to apply it faithfully while you are in the sun.

If you do get too much sun, there are a number of home remedies that can take the sting out of burned skin: diluted vinegar, yogurt, buttermilk, club soda, baking soda, mashed fresh tomatoes, lard, and cocoa butter are all soothing.

Hands and Nails

Your hands attract almost as much attention as your face. The skin is vulnerable, and unless you're a lady of leisure, your hands take a daily beating. They are in and out of water and detergents. They get dirty and sometimes stained. They get chapped from the cold, and chapped skin is often broken and likely to pick up infections. They are said to be the first part of a woman's body to show signs of age.

Old-time beauty columnists used to suggest applying heavy coatings of oil or grease to the hands at night and going to bed with gloves or mittens on to keep from buttering up the sheets. It's still good advice, but it's necessary only as a last resort when your hands are really a mess. If you get in the habit of rubbing in a little oil or lotion (your own mix or a commercial brand) every time you've had your hands in water, you won't need to resort to the mitten treatment.

GLYCERIN AND ROSEWATER   Your great-grandmothers swore by this combination. Buy it ready-mixed from the druggist or mix it yourself, equal parts of each. Rub a bit on your hands every time you've had them in water. You can also use straight glycerin. However, it takes time to work it into the skin, and some people say it makes their hands rough and red.

GLYCERIN AND LEMON JUICE   A mixture of equal parts of these ingredients will take the smell of garlic or onions off your fingers as well as soften your skin. Lemon juice alone will eliminate the odor.

POTATO   To remove stains from your hands, cut a raw potato in half and rub the cut side over the stains.

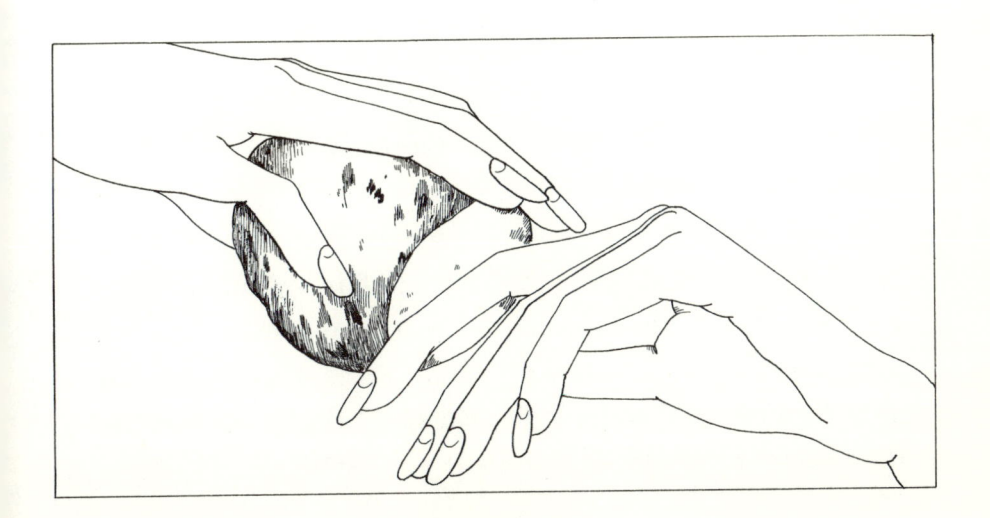

OATMEAL OR CORNMEAL If you've been working in the garden or tuning up your bicycle, add a little of either (raw, of course) to the lather of your soap to clean your hands and soften them.

FATS AND OILS Butter, margarine, cocoa butter, and olive oil are greasy, but all are good for your hands.

Fingernails are made up of dead cells, but they are excellent indicators of your general state of health. The bumps, ridges, and white spots that show up are a sign of your health and of your diet when the nail was forming. Doctors can diagnose some diseases by examining nails.

The standard advice for people with poor nails is to mix gelatin, a protein, with water or fruit juice and to drink a daily dose of it. Some dermatologists say there is no value to this remedy. But perhaps you want to make up your own mind: try it for a few weeks and see. Gelatin can't hurt you, and it might help your nails.

The cuticle, the hardened strip of skin around the base of the nail, can be pushed back. Cutting it or removing it chemically can cause problems, such as infections.

Feet have not attracted the same attention as hands, for obvious reasons, with the exception of the ancient Oriental practice of binding women's feet to keep them tiny and virtually useless. But modern feet are often encased in shoes that are quite cruel to hard-walking, long-standing feet. If they develop calluses, you can soften the toughened layers of skin by rubbing them with wet salt or with a pumice stone. Treat them regularly—especially the heels—to whatever emollient you favor.

HAIR AND OTHER GLORIES

Saint Paul was so intrigued with women's hair that he ordered them to cover their heads in church so as not to tempt the devil—and possibly weak-willed saints. The French philosopher Voltaire once wrote that no woman can be bad looking with good teeth and good looking with bad ones. Shakespeare, writing about a woman, could hardly take his eyes off her eyes. In order to keep saints, philosophers, poets, and more ordinary men gazing in admiration, women have always devoted much attention to maintaining these glories.

The Natural Crown

Your hair and how you fix it tell more about you than any other physical characteristic, and this has been true of both males and females in every known culture. Hair indicates age, social position, political attitudes, and usually sex. Young men have found themselves out of jobs or in jail because of what people believe their hair shows about them. And, as with other marks of beauty, what you have is seldom what you want. People with curly hair often go to great trouble to straighten it; people with straight hair take pains to curl it. When hair turns white, people darken it with dye. If it's too dark, they bleach it.

When it falls out, or when it's not the right length, color, or curl, they put on wigs. Changing your hairstyle is the quickest and easiest way to create a new appearance. Wigs make the change easy and less drastic.

Each hair grows from a tiny pouch in the skin called a follicle. The scalp has about 1000 hair follicles per square inch, giving you between 100,000 and 140,000 hairs on your head, depending on whether your hair is dark or light. Dark hairs are coarser than light hairs, and there tend to be fewer of them. Hair cells form at the bottom of each follicle, sticking together, overlapping, and hardening as they are pushed up and out at the rate of about one-half inch a month. Each follicle also contains an oil gland to lubricate the hair. When the hair gets to be about two or three feet long, it becomes too heavy for the root to hold, falls out, and is replaced by a new hair. The color, texture, and curliness of the hair produced by each follicle is determined by heredity.

About half of the seven billion dollars spent each year on beauty in the United States is handed over to hairdressers, and another big chunk goes to purchase shampoos, rinses, lotions, and dyes to use at home. Although hair, unlike skin, is dead, it requires careful handling, as though it were delicate fabric.

Washing

Before the 1930's, people washed their hair with ordinary soap, which left a rather dull film on it, usually from a reaction with minerals in the water. Shampoos are an offshoot of the development of synthetic detergents.

They leave the hair shiny, but they also strip away all the natural oil and make hair dry and brittle. If you want to avoid detergent shampoos, wash your hair with a mild soap and rinse it thoroughly with plain water, followed by a rinse of lemon juice or vinegar solution to remove the dull film.

BLONDE RINSE Lemon juice is a mild bleach that will bring out the highlights of light hair. It also helps to cut down on oiliness. Squeeze a lemon, strain the juice, and mix it with a cup of water. Pour it through your hair after you have washed and rinsed it completely with plain water. Catch the lemon rinse in a glass, enamel, or ceramic bowl, and pour it through your hair a second time. Rinse with more plain water.

BRUNETTE RINSE Mix two tablespoons of vinegar with a pint of water, and pour it through your hair several times, catching it in a nonmetallic bowl. If you wait a bit, the vinegary smell will go away by itself; if it bothers you, rinse it out with plain water.

Conditioning

Many people use hair conditioners when they wash their hair. Some conditioners on the market claim to include protein, such as dehydrated egg powder. Since everybody knows that protein is an essential body builder, the theory is that protein in a conditioner can "feed" the hair. It doesn't, though; hair is already dead and can't be nourished or revitalized. However, protein conditioners do stick to the individual hairs, coating them with a residue that gives the hair more body and makes it easier to manage. They won't heal damaged hair; trim your hair every few weeks to remove split ends and to keep it from breaking and splitting more.

There has always been a preoccupation (among women) with making hair grow long and (among men) with keeping it from falling out. Just as people have smeared all manner of things on their faces in the name of beautiful skin, they have anointed their heads with all sorts of preparations including (but not limited to) bear grease, beef marrow, skunk oil, fox grease, butter, and a mixture of honey and lye made from the roots of various vegetables. Here are two alternatives.

MAYONNAISE   Rub a little, straight from the jar, on the ends of your hair, and then rinse it out.

OLIVE OIL   Although this oil is the traditional conditioner for dry hair, it sometimes causes more problems than it solves. If you have a dry, flaky scalp, oil can make it worse. Yet many beauty experts still recommend it for people whose hair is extremely dry from too much sun and swimming. Rub a very small amount of oil into your scalp and through your hair. Then soak a towel in very warm water, wring it out, and wrap it around your head. (Some say to use hot water to steam the hair; warm water is much gentler.) When the towel is cool, wet it again. Do this four times. Then wash your hair. You may have to soap and rinse several times to get rid of the excess oil. Finish with a vinegar rinse.

There are a number of effective antidandruff shampoos available, but they are usually strong detergents that are drying to the hair, and some people are allergic to them. For a home remedy, apply a mixture of equal parts vinegar and water directly to the scalp with cotton balls. Then wash and finish with a vinegar rinse.

Brushing

Brushing your hair distributes the oil from the roots over the whole length of the hair and keeps it soft and shining. It also helps to remove dust that naturally collects in the hair. In great-grandmother's time, girls were advised to brush their hair a hundred strokes a day. But recent evidence seems to show that such brushing is not only unnecessary, it is hard on the hair. Whether you go in for marathon brushing or not, you should invest in a good natural-bristle brush rather than a nylon one. (The natural bristles don't have sharp ends that can damage your hair.) Wash the brush regularly in a solution of ammonia and water or in water with baking soda added.

Never brush your hair when it is wet. Wet hair is much more fragile and likely to break than dry hair. Rub it nearly dry with a towel before you begin to brush it into a style. Heat makes hair dry and brittle; if you use a dryer, a cool setting is much better for your hair, even if it takes longer for it to dry.

Curling and Straightening

Women with straight hair have always desired curls. In ancient Egypt they used wet mud to set their hair; in comparatively modern times they soaked quince seeds in water and combed the thick jelly that formed through their hair as a setting lotion. Not too many years ago women rinsed their hair with beer to give it more body and ability to hold curl. It also gave it a barroom odor and a sticky feeling. Eventually a chemical was found that would change the physical structure of the hair shaft, and in the 1930's the permanent wave was invented. Less drastic devices for curling the hair have included hot curlers and curling irons, bobby pins for tight little curls, plastic rollers for big loose ones, blowers for practically no curl. All have been in and out of fashion, and all have caused damage to the hair by weakening it or breaking it.

Meanwhile, women with extremely curly hair have longed to have it straight. For a long time black women (and men) straightened their naturally frizzy hair by a variety of processes: pomade, a greasy substance that temporarily flattened out the curl, or heat or chemicals to relax the curl permanently. When attitudes and styles changed, frizzy, natural hair became a mark of pride in one's racial background, and the Afro was born. Then black women revived the art of cornrowing, an elaborate style of plaiting the hair originally brought from Africa and quietly passed down through generations of black Americans until actress Cicily Tyson made cornrowing high fashion.

Whether curled or straightened, there was the problem of keeping styled hair in place. Hair sprays that slightly stiffen the hair have replaced old-fashioned hair lacquers containing shellac that made a hairdo as rigid as plastic.

Bleaching and Dyeing

Although blond hair was the sign of a prostitute in ancient Greece and Rome, at other times it has been associated with innocence and femininity. Consequently, people have bleached their hair at different times and for different reasons.

In the late 1800's it was discovered that hydrogen peroxide would take the color out of hair, turning it the strawlike yellow that marked its users as "bottle blondes." About a quarter of American women were blond as children, but most of them darken as they grow older. Only a few adults are true blondes; others have their hair made blond professionally. First the color is stripped out of the hair with bleach; then it is "toned" by dyeing in a more subtle shade.

If blond hair is highly desirable in our culture, white hair is not, because it is almost always associated with aging. When the individual cell that produces the pigment for each hair stops functioning, the hair that grows from that follicle has no color; it is white. As more and more of these white hairs accumulate, it looks as though the hair is turning gray. Only when the white hairs have almost completely replaced the pigmented hairs does the hair look truly white. The age at which a person's hair turns gray is usually determined by heredity, although there are sometimes stories about people whose hair has allegedly turned white overnight, usually as the result of some sudden shock. Such overnight change is impossible, because pigmented hair cannot lose its pigment. Even if all the pigment cells stop working at the same moment, it still takes months for the new, uncolored hair to replace the old, colored hair.

People who were satisfied with their natural hair color may start to dye their hair as they get older. This was true even in Roman times, when people dipped a lead comb in vinegar and passed it through their hair, depositing lead salts on the hair that gradually darkened it. Using a special lotion, this method is still both valid and popular, especially among men. However, it's incompatible with permanent-wave chemicals, so few women choose to use it.

In ancient Egypt, dark-haired women colored their hair with henna, the dried and powdered leaves of a certain plant that yields a permanent reddish dye. Recently there has been a revival of interest in henna by advocates of natural cosmetics. The problem is that auburn is the only color obtainable, and that shade varies considerably, depending on the color of the hair to start with. Messy to use, henna dyes the keratin in your fingernails as well as your hair.

Many of the dyes used in hair coloring can cause severe allergic reactions. If you decide to dye your hair, you must do a patch test first, putting a few drops of the solution on the sensitive skin on the inside of your elbow or behind your ear. Leave it undisturbed for a day or two.

If your skin becomes red and irritated, you should not use that dye. Most state laws require patch testing by beauty salons, but in practice few obey the law. All products for home use carry warnings and directions for the test. It must be repeated every time the dye is used, since there is a buildup of sensitivity. The same product might be used several times with no sign of reaction and a severe reaction the next time. None of these dyes should ever be used on eyebrows or eyelashes, for they may cause injury or even blindness.

There are several reasons not to dye your hair. Dyeing and bleaching make it dry and brittle. And permanent hair coloring is a major commitment that needs regular attention to keep your hair attractive. Hair grows at the rate of about a half inch per month, which seems very fast when you must have the roots touched up to match the rest of the hair (and a patch test first). But it seems very slow indeed when you are waiting for the dyed hair to grow out and be replaced with your own natural color.

An alternative for the less committed or more cautious is a temporary rinse that merely covers the outer surface layer of the hair but doesn't change the natural color pigment inside the shaft. You can't go from dark to light with a rinse, although you can brighten up dull hair. Rinses, too, require patch testing before you use them.

Wigs

Far worse than having the wrong color or curl in your hair is having no hair or not enough of it. Some hair loss is caused by illness, but most baldness, common among white males, is hereditary. The hair falls out, never to be replaced, in a pattern that is passed along genetically. Many men used to conceal their bald spots with partial wigs called "toupees" and hope that no one would notice. Although wigs have been in and out of fashion through the ages for both sexes, in the past century they've been demanded mostly by bald men, theater people, and Orthodox Jewish women as a matter of religious tradition. But starting in the late 1950's, wigs began to be part of the scheme of anyone—male or female—who wanted to look like a totally different person or a better version of the same person. Between 1960 and 1970, the wig business grew more than a thousand percent.

Wigs are made from synthetic hair or from real hair imported mostly from the Orient, collected from temples where it is offered as a sacrifice. But since Oriental hair is much different from what most Americans have or want—blacker, straighter, coarser—the hair is stripped of its color, dyed in an assortment of shades from chestnut through flaming red to ash blond, stitched to a backing, permanently curled, and eventually styled to suit the new owner. But a wig isn't always convenient. A real-hair wig must be sent out to a hairdresser to be cleaned and set, although less real-looking synthetics can be washed at home and don't need setting. Wigs aren't perfect; they're hot in the summer, unsuitable for swimming, and they sometimes come off at the most awkward moment. Despite the drawbacks, some women own a complete wardrobe of wigs to suit the mood, occasion, and costume.

Body Hair

What's admired on the head is not always desired elsewhere on the body. Most Americans, both male and female, have been brought up to believe that body hair on women is animallike and, therefore, unattractive. Not all cultures share this view. In some European countries, for instance, leg hair and underarm hair are completely acceptable and considered more attractive than the sleek hairlessness that seems to deny one's animal nature and sexuality. But in the United States, body hair is out (except among some ethnic groups and among some feminists who see hair removal as another symbol of male domination). Most women start to get rid of leg and underarm hair almost as soon as it sprouts, either by shaving or by using hair removers called "depilatories," another product in existence since Cleopatra was a girl. A simple and safe depilatory was—and still is—wax. A coating of warm liquid wax is applied to the skin; the wax hardens, imbedding the hairs. When you pull off the wax, much like stripping off an adhesive bandage and just as uncomfortable, the hairs come, too. The method requires some bravery.

Chemical depilatories are painless but potentially dangerous, if you happen to be sensitive to the ingredients. Like permanent-waving lotions, chemical depilatories weaken the structure of the hair. In the waving process this weakening is controlled and then reversed, but a depilatory allows the hair to be weakened so much that it easily breaks off at the surface of the skin and can be washed away. Like shaving, a depilatory is a way to remove hair only temporarily, although it breaks the hair closer to the skin than shaving does and, therefore, takes longer to grow back. Despite what you may have heard, shaving doesn't make the hairs coarser or increase the number of them. Low-dosage X-raying is another way to remove hair temporarily; a dosage high enough to destroy the hair-forming cells also destroys the normal skin around it.

Facial hair on a woman—on the upper lip, for instance—is considered much too masculine-looking in most cultures. The only safe way to remove it permanently is by professionally performed electrolysis, in which a fine wire is inserted into each individual hair follicle and an electric current passed through the wire to kill the cells that form the hair. Although electrolysis is expensive, it is safer than bleaches or other temporary chemical methods.

Teeth

The expression "good teeth" hasn't always meant the same thing to everybody. The Egyptians flashed smiles brightened by red ocher; in some parts of the Orient people still find blackened teeth quite charming. Until recent times people usually lost their teeth, whatever the color, at an early age. But today the big white healthy smile is in fashion.

Not surprisingly, manufacturers of toothpaste and mouthwash have gone out of their way to make Americans conscious of their mouths. Centuries ago people made tooth powder of pumice, a porous volcanic rock, that not only did an excellent job of removing stains and tartar from teeth but took off most of the enamel. You can buy toothpaste in assorted flavors containing ingredients meant to retard tooth decay and to sweeten the breath. You can also make a safe, simple tooth cleaner yourself.

TOOTH POWDER   A mixture of equal parts of table salt and baking soda cleans your teeth, takes away stains from various foods such as the tannic acid in tea and the iron in spinach, and acts as a mild antiseptic to help prevent the formation of tartar. If the mixture is too Spartan for your taste, add some finely grated lemon rind.

Most authorities believe that mouthwash serves very little purpose. It is not an effective way to kill germs, and a much better approach is to keep teeth clean by brushing them regularly, soon after eating. Persistent bad breath may be a sign of tooth decay or other physical problems. It hasn't been proved that any mouthwash can eliminate cold germs.

PARSLEY   If you want to improve your breath, here's an old remedy. Parsley is loaded with natural chlorophyll and has a fresh, pleasant scent of its own. Chew a sprig; then rinse your mouth with plain water.

Eyes

Probably the most romantic part of the body, the eyes have been described in a number of poetic phrases, such as the windows of the soul and the jewels of the face.

Belladonna, extracted from the leaves and roots of the deadly nightshade, dilates the pupils of the eyes. Women once used it to make their eyes look larger and darker (*belladonna* means "beautiful lady" in Italian). Other determined and unflinching souls used to squirt lemon juice in their eyes to make them sparkle, a rather extreme beauty treatment that starts tears flowing just at the thought of it.

The idea generally is to soothe the eyes, not to irritate them. Some people use commercial eye-drop preparations, many of which contain boric acid. You can mix your own solution to treat your eyes when they're irritated by dust or allergens.

BORIC-ACID EYEWASH Dissolve a teaspoonful of powdered boric acid in a cup of boiled water. When it is cool, use it to wash your eyes with an eye cup or with cotton balls soaked in the solution. Mix a fresh batch every time you use it to avoid contamination.

If your eyes are tired and puffy, try this old, gentle prescription:

TEA-BAG TREATMENT Lie down with wet tea bags (or cotton balls dipped in weak tea) placed on your eyelids for ten or fifteen minutes. The tannic acid in the tea is soothing, and you'll feel refreshed and bright-eyed again.

PART TWO
Making Up

At different periods throughout history women, and sometimes men, have painted their faces a lot, or a little, or not at all. In an almost predictably regular pattern, attitudes toward makeup have ranged from total acceptance to complete rejection and back again. The earliest face painting was for purposes of magic and religion. Only later was it for purposes of being beautiful.

Cleopatra, probably the most famous of all cosmetics users, was typical of Egyptian women of her time, who were very sophisticated in their use of cosmetics. Some of the ones they used have been found, well preserved, in the luxurious tombs of Egyptian kings. The Egyptians were experts in eye makeup, aware that the quickest way to change one's face is by emphasizing the most dramatic feature. Cleopatra painted her eyes with kohl made from powdered antimony, black on the lids and green or blue below the eyes, and she thickened her lashes and brows with more kohl.

Ovid, the Roman poet of the same era who wrote extensively about love, believed that some kind of artificial painting was necessary for beauty and offered this advice: "Rouge a pale cheek, a red one powder. Each maiden knows that art's allowed." Ovid went on to recommend white lead as the best substance for powdering the too-red cheek. Poppaea, Nero's infamous wife, used a mixture of white lead and refined grease to whiten her skin. Although she survived her makeup (but not Nero's treatment of her), countless women throughout history who followed such advice have died of lead poisoning.

Between the time of the Egyptian queen of two thousand years ago and the woman of today, styles in painting have changed often and drastically. At one time women plucked their eyebrows and shaved off the hair above their foreheads to make their faces as blank and uninteresting as possible; they drew attention instead toward their bosoms. At other times, women pasted little patches on their faces to make their lips or eyes more noticeable. As is true of almost every kind of makeup, this technique sometimes went to extremes. Imagine the detailed silhouette of a coach and four horses prancing across a woman's cheek!

During the reign of Queen Elizabeth I of England in the sixteenth century, makeup came into obvious use. As the queen got older, she put a red wig on her head and more and more makeup on her face. But by the eighteenth century, attitudes had changed again. Parliament passed a bill stating that "all women, regardless of age, rank, or status, who seduced or betrayed into matrimony any of his Majesty's subjects by the use of perfume, paints, artificial teeth, wigs, stays, hoops, high-heeled shoes" and so on might not only find their marriage annulled, they might find themselves subject to punishment for witchcraft.

The young colony of Pennsylvania adopted a similar law. The New England Puritans objected to cosmetics on moral grounds. In fact, cosmetics did not fare at all well in the New World, and there was heavy social pressure against the use of makeup. Whatever beautifiers were used during the early days of America were homemade and probably did little more than moisturize the skin. There was no painting—only women of bad reputation did that—but most women pinched their cheeks and bit their lips for whatever color they could get. More daring women rubbed their faces with bits of red ribbon and secretly prepared lip salves from crushed rose petals, although most would have swooned rather than own up to the deceit. The more adventuresome traced the veins on their chest and arms with blue powder.

Even at the end of the nineteenth century, women were still using skin-care products for "health" and not —at least admittedly—for beauty. Eventually a few of the bolder women, the kind who are the first to try a new fashion, began to use some subtle makeup. Others followed. When the practice became widespread, the innovators moved on to try something more outrageous. But not until well into this century did the use of cosmetics become as open as it was in ancient Egypt.

PIONEERING WOMEN

Although there have always been makers and sellers of beauty preparations whenever cosmetics were widely used, most women concocted their own. When painting was frowned upon, the business simply went underground. Then as certain creams for complexion care (for "health," of course) were accepted, the makers and sellers cautiously emerged again.

Harriet Hubbard Ayer was the first to start a cosmetics business in the United States. She had lived grandly and traveled widely until she was divorced from her wealthy husband. When her former husband lost his fortune, Mrs. Ayer had to scramble to support herself and her children. Eventually she became a successful importer of antiques. On a buying trip to Paris in 1886, she had a chemist prepare some face cream for her and was so pleased with it that she bought the prescription. Guessing that times were changing, Mrs. Ayer borrowed $50,000 and wrote an advertisement for the cream, inventing the story that it was a secret cream once used by the famous French beauty, Mme. Récamier. Although it couldn't be stated in the advertisement that this was a beauty cream intended to make the user more attractive to men, that was the implication behind the story. After the success of the Mme. Récamier tale, Mrs. Ayer went on to recruit other well-known and beautiful women to endorse her products.

About this time, Helena Rubinstein emigrated from her native Poland to Australia, taking with her a dozen jars of her mother's complexion cream. The Australians were much impressed by Helena's beautiful skin, and she began to write home for more cream. As demand exceeded supply, she borrowed money to open a salon. With the help of the chemist who had formulated her mother's cream with herbs and almond essence, she began making and selling compounds for different skin types. Painting was still out of favor, but the demand for "medicated" skin creams never waned.

This was only the beginning for Rubinstein. In the early 1900's women would dust on a touch of rice powder that coated the skin like whitewash, but it also swelled in the pores of the skin and clogged them. Rubinstein solved one problem by making up a tinted powder that would be less obvious and, therefore, more acceptable, if no kinder to pores. At that time only actresses had the know-how and skill for painting. From them she learned the art of using eye shadow and passed it on to her clients. In 1915, after her initial success with the Australians and later with the British, Rubinstein arrived in New York. By 1920, she had salons all over the world. Helena Rubinstein had 629 items in her cosmetics line, including 115 lipsticks, but reportedly she used few of them herself. Calling herself the world's greatest beauty culturist, she amassed a fortune of over five hundred million dollars.

But she was by no means alone in this burgeoning industry. Among the early competitors was Chesebrough-Ponds, makers of Vaseline petroleum jelly. They advertised their product on the sides of horse buses and trolley cars until it became a household word; women used it on their chapped lips and liked the shine. Early in the century Ponds decided to capitalize on their knowledge and well-known name to produce face creams and lotions as well. Yardley, an English soap manufacturer established in 1770, expanded by introducing a line of toilet water, a mild cologne.

Mme. Rubinstein's arch rival was Elizabeth Arden, the daughter of a poor Canadian truck driver. According to *Fortune* magazine, Arden probably earned more money than any other businesswoman in history. And, of course, many others joined the ranks. Most folded; a few became giants: Revlon, Hazel Bishop, Max Factor, and Estée Lauder. Today the largest cosmetics company in the world is Avon, and it reached its size by selling its products door-to-door.

PAINTING IN THE TWENTIETH CENTURY

At the beginning of the century, the emphasis was on beauty through health. Although many respectable women used rouge, few dared admit it; for years only prostitutes had painted openly, and the association could be dreadfully embarrassing. Lip salve was the least acceptable of all cosmetics used, and eye shadow was unmentionable. Obviously somebody was making up, though, because the first lipsticks and eyebrow pencils were manufactured in America about 1915.

Not until after World War I did painting begin to gain acceptance among Americans. More women had money to spend on the cosmetics that were inexpensive and available in most stores. A double standard persisted: well-to-do women were free to experiment with cosmetics, but working girls—servants, clerks, office workers—often lost their jobs or were at least severely criticized if they used makeup.

By the 1920's, makeup was generally allowed, if it were applied so expertly that it was not obvious. The natural look, however it was achieved, was still absolutely essential. Men who suspected that their womenfolk applied makeup made their objections known, but eventually even that changed.

As the years passed, the infant cosmetics industry grew, not only in dollar volume, but in the variety of products offered. There was a time, for instance, when green-tinted face powder was in vogue, because the wearers were convinced it made them look "interesting." Eventually brighter complexions—described as the "suntanned look" —came into fashion, and the white-powdered faces with balloons of red rouge went out of style.

Lipsticks were made to match nail polish, and the range of shades available expanded from the standard choices of light, medium, and dark to an eye-glazing array. Beauty experts evolved different styles of makeup for day and for evening. Although some people still objected to the use of cosmetics on moral grounds, more converts were won over as the quality of the cosmetics improved and they became safer and easier to use.

Just as makeup was coming into its own, World War II broke out. There were shortages to deal with, mostly with containers: metal was needed to make bullets, not lipstick cases; glass was expensive; plastic was scarce. But it didn't take long to discover that once-despised cosmetics were now essential morale builders and that, in fact, lipsticks were essential to the war effort. Both manufacturers and customers made do until peace came again. By then everyone understood the great psychological value of makeup.

Film stars had enormous influence on cosmetics in the 1930's and 1940's. So did the invention of Technicolor movies, in which women could see not only the shape of a cupid's-bow mouth but the shade worn by the leading lady. Max Factor, a Hollywood cosmetician who created "makeup for the stars," gave the world the first commercial pancake makeup. (Oriental women had traditionally made cakes of dried rice powder, which they smeared on their faces with pieces of wet cloth.)

In the early 1950's, eye makeup became as important as lipstick, and styles came and went as quick as a wink. Eyeliners were used to match and eventually to outdo Cleopatra and her kohl stick. Women painted their eyes to look Oriental, Egyptian, or deerlike.

About the same time, one of the most famous campaigns in advertising history was launched when Revlon introduced a new lipstick and nail polish called Fire and Ice. A magazine advertisement, featuring a beautiful model in silver sequins and red cape, and a catchy questionnaire ("Do you close your eyes when you're kissed? Do you think any man *really* understands you? Have you ever danced with your shoes off?") sent millions of women out to buy the bright-red lipstick, whether it suited their individual coloring or not. Apparently every female wanted to see herself as a Fire and Ice woman. This heralded a new era in advertising. Quality of product was no longer enough; makeup had to be sexy and glamorous. The name of the lipstick was no longer a description of its color but a promise of excitement and allure.

Another approach was taken by Avon, which exchanged glamour for the neighborliness of ordinary women knocking on doors.

During that same decade, even nice girls began to color

their hair, convinced at least in part by Clairol's clever advertising. Hair spray was invented to keep hair in its place. Miracle creams containing cheap ingredients were sold at high prices, bringing hope to worried women and riches to clever businessmen.

Late in the 1960's, women took a lesson from stage makeup and began to "contour" their faces with highlights and shadows supplied by light and dark paint to give the illusion of more interesting bone structure. The natural look came and went, but always with a host of products that were necessary to provide what nature failed to give.

In the 1970's an old idea became new again—that beauty comes from within, the result of proper diet. As natural foods became a fad, so did natural cosmetics, using organic ingredients that had been around for generations before chemists took over. Experts debated whether "natural" was necessarily better than "synthetic." There seemed to be scientific evidence on both sides. But women loved the idea, and so, of course, did the cosmetics companies that immediately brought out a new line of products containing strawberries, avocados, cucumbers, and so on. One pharmacologist, searching for ways to make cosmetics safe and believing that if you could eat it you could safely wear it, concocted a liquid makeup from chocolate syrup and mashed potatoes. Many women enthusiastically smeared themselves with cucumber juice and sliced tomatoes, but that particular chocolate sundae never aroused much of a following.

Sometime during the growing years of the cosmetics industry, a subtle change took place. The industry got its start by giving women what they wanted; changes and improvements came about because the trend setters and their followers demanded them. But then power began to shift. Today women are told by the manufacturers—through advertising and the beauty and fashion magazines working closely with them—what cosmetics they will use and what styles they will follow. The industry, not the consumer, creates the demand.

As fads and fashions in makeup bloom and fade, women buy what they are taught to want—relatively inexpensive products that make them feel better. They rarely use up what they buy before the next shade or style is introduced, and a stockpile of cosmetics accumulates. The possibility of glamour is within the reach of everyone.

What's in Those Jars?

The question of what cosmetics are made of apparently doesn't matter to most people. But there is a growing number of consumers who are concerned with the safety of the products they use, who question the miraculous claims of the manufacturers, and who protest the wide gap between the cost of making the product and the price at which it is sold.

When Senator Maurine B. Neuberger of Oregon was co-sponsoring a "truth in packaging" bill in Congress in 1965, she claimed that two thirds of the cost of cosmetics went into packaging, advertising, and promotion, and that very little was actually spent on ingredients. But it took ten years until consumer pressure finally helped to force enactment of a law that requires cosmetic manufacturers to list the ingredients on the label in descending order of quantity used.

The industry fought this labeling law long and hard, at least partly because water is the principal ingredient in most cosmetics. (Food manufacturers, who must state what goes into their canned soups and stews, objected to the same kind of labeling law for the same reasons and with the same results.) It seems a foolish objection; most consumers ignore the label and buy what they've been conditioned to want.

Nevertheless, despite the wholehearted efforts of the cosmetics industry, the Food and Drug Administration (FDA) announced that any cosmetic manufactured after March 31, 1975, must list the ingredients on the label, using commonly understood terms. Manufacturers had until the end of that year to sell or get rid of their unlabeled products.

If you're a label reader, here are a few common ingredients you may find listed among the welter of polysyllables:

Lecithin A common substance found in all plant and animal tissues, the word means "egg yolk." A good emollient, it also aids in keeping emulsions of oil and water from separating.

Tincture of benzoin An ingredient often called for in

homemade cosmetics as a preservative, it's not used in hypoallergenic cosmetics because many people are sensitive to it.

Casein The principal protein of cow's milk is commonly included as the "protein" ingredient in shampoos and hair conditioners.

Citric acid The acid in lemon juice is one of the most common in cosmetics manufacturing.

Propylene glycol A humectant, like glycerin, it keeps creams smooth and spreadable.

"Hope is what we sell..."

Even with the improved law, consumer groups are still not satisfied, and a kind of war has sprung up between the realists and the romantics. The realists are looking for dollar value; they are angered that the cost of materials of a lipstick that sells for more than two dollars is less than twenty-five cents. And much of that cost of materials goes for packaging; the ingredients of the lipstick itself cost next to nothing.

Most lipsticks are made of castor oil and beeswax, a combination that makes them stiff enough to hold their shape in the tube but soft enough to spread smoothly on the lips; perfume and flavoring to disguise the natural odor and taste; color pigment. Simple as that recipe seems, it and all others have been guarded fanatically by the manufacturers. Revlon, for example, gives a code name to all products before they are introduced. Although the labeling law may have changed the practice, manufacturers used to code the names of ingredients, too. Only a few people knew what the code stood for; workers in the factory theoretically had no idea what they were mixing or even exactly what they were making. Not that there was much variation in formulas from company to company. When one company introduced a new product—frosted lipsticks made with fish scales, for instance—all the others quickly followed. The big difference has always been the package and the advertising pitch.

The vast spectrum of lipstick shades remains much the same, although the names of the colors change. Periodically old ones are reactivated with new names coined to conjure up fantasies of romance and glamour. Fresh advertising campaigns are launched with fanfare, to attract new customers and keep old ones interested.

Charles Revson, the powerful and flamboyant founder of Revlon who died in 1975, operated on the theory that if he kept his manufacturing costs low enough, he could afford to advertise heavily. And instead of lowering prices to beat the competition, he *raised* them. Advertising and distribution are the largest costs in any cosmetic product, amounting to perhaps as much as 80 percent of the company's budget. Only a few products are big sellers. About a fifth of those put on the market actually find enough customers to make it worthwhile to continue producing them. The profit from a few successes covers the cost of many failures.

One way to reduce the numbers of failures is by careful psychological research of both product and advertising. It's important for manufacturers to know, for example, that women over twenty-five prefer pink hand lotion while teen-agers reach for blue, and they hire a research organization to dig out that fact for them. Ad agencies must be just as careful to find out how women feel about themselves. The advertising for hair coloring is a case in point. Back in the 1950's, ads picturing a mother and child helped to assure people that even *nice* women dye their hair. And the ads for a dye that covers gray hair show only young-looking women; advertisers know that middle-aged women want to identify with youth rather than with middle age.

If advertising is the most important (and costly) ingredient in a product from the manufacturer's point of view, then belief that it will work is the most important from the user's point of view. Advertising creates that belief. Said one industry official, "Hope is what we sell in cosmetics."

Customers for cosmetics and for the hope they seem to offer are created at an early age. By the time you are in your teens, you already know a great deal about makeup styles. Beauty columnists in the magazines you read tell you what you should be doing to make yourself look beautiful, and the advertisements present you with pictures of the not-quite-impossible ideal. A young girl and her mother probably don't read the same magazines, but they do get the same message, over and over: beauty is a ritual, and if the reader faithfully follows the prescription, doing the right things and using the right products in the right way, she too can become beautiful. And being beautiful means that people will be attracted to you; women and girls will admire and perhaps envy you; men and boys will fall madly in love with you.

The right cosmetics may indeed fulfill all your dreams. And then again they may give you a rash—or worse.

Danger! Beautifiers!

Women have literally killed themselves trying to be beautiful. Hundreds—perhaps thousands—died from powdering their faces with white lead. An epidemic of poisonings raged through Europe in the seventeenth century, taking the lives of women who used a "beauty wash" containing arsenic. In that century when Italy required the registration of all poisonous substances, a precedent was set for modern cosmetic laws.

When the cosmetics industry was still young, manufacturers were not careful with their formulations. Although harmful ingredients were not knowingly used, no one bothered with testing. There was no government regulation. In the 1930's an eyelash dye caused blindness, disfigurement, and death, but even after the cases had received wide public attention, the product was not withdrawn from the market. Finally the Food, Drug, and Cosmetic Act of 1938 was passed, but it specifically excluded soap—an example of what industry pressure can accomplish.

The law was on the books, but with few teeth it had a not especially fearsome bite. There were light penalties ($1000 fine for the first offense, $10,000 for the second—a small expense for the businessmen who run the companies) for "adulteration," a difficult charge to prove. Pretesting was not required; although most reputable companies did test their products, a few, out to make a quick killing at the customer's expense, did not. And the manufacturer did not have to list his ingredients.

Allergies

Just how much danger lurked in the unlabeled cosmetics depends on whose report you read. Certainly until the passage of the 1938 law, which also banned coal-tar dyes from most cosmetics, there were real dangers. Since then the main problem with cosmetics has been allergies. Sixty ingredients, including cornstarch, gum arabic, and oil of spearmint, are well-known allergens—substances that cause allergic reactions in many people. One of the principal allergens is the perfume used to mask the unpleasant odor of the ingredients in many products. Manufacturers who have eliminated the perfume and other well-known allergens call their products "hypoallergenic," a term that means they are least likely to cause a reaction. There is no such thing as a nonallergenic product, because there is always somebody who is allergic to something.

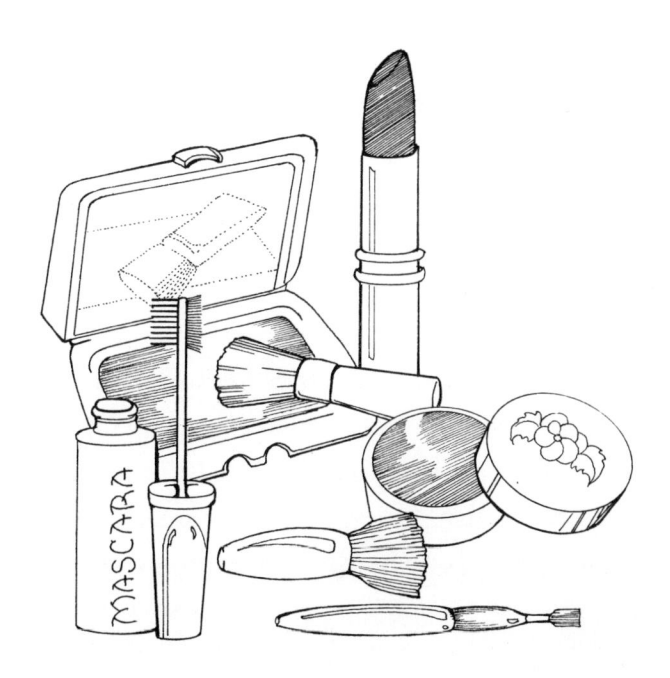

The cosmetics that cause the most problems are eye makeup. Because the eyes are extremely sensitive, products used near them must be free of allergens and of contamination. Although eye cosmetics are uncontaminated when you buy them, keeping them that way is difficult. Since pencils, brushes, and other tools used to apply the makeup easily pick up and harbor bacteria and transfer it to the product, doctors suggest discarding supplies after a couple of months and buying new ones. For obvious reasons, eye makeup should be waterproof, which makes it hard to remove. Mineral oil is the best solvent for taking it off.

Not long after the 1938 law was passed, a writer for the cosmetics industry claimed that the belief that cosmetic caused allergies was unfounded. He wrote that the number of complaints proving to be actually due to cosmetics was "infinitely small" compared to the amount of cosmetics sold.

Much more recently a dermatologist asserted in his book, "There is no safety problem of any real consequence," estimating that the actual number of reactions to cosmetics products is about 10,000 a year, one out of 20,000 people, a rate far lower than the number of reactions to strawberries, shellfish, and other known allergens. The real problems, he believes, are ineffective products and consumer frauds.

But in 1972 the President's National Commission on Product Safety issued a report setting the number of people who suffer from skin eruptions, burns, itching, loss of hair, and other allergic reactions at about 60,000 a year. It's hard to determine an accurate number, because most people don't report to their doctors whether a moisturizer makes their skin break out or a face powder makes them sneeze. Furthermore, it's not always easy to tell what's causing an allergic reaction. Sensitivity to certain ingredients in nail polish, to cite an extreme example, doesn't show up in the nails or hands but in the *eyelids*.

One class of products that has brought many complaints is the vaginal deodorant. In 1966, working on the American woman's obsessive worry about smells, the cosmetics industry began promoting "feminine hygiene sprays." Soon reports of irritation, bladder infections, and so on began to pile up in the offices of the Food and Drug Administration. Some blamed the problem on the aerosol propellants, which can be extremely drying and irritating to delicate tissues. Many doctors advised their patients to go back to plain soap and water. Then the manufacturer of a much-advertised spray conducted tests and announced that soap-and-water users had more problems than women who sprayed with their product. Suspecting that the test may not have been entirely unbiased, doctors continue to recommend bathing.

Testing ought, of course, to be done long before the product ever reaches the shelves. And usually it is. Technicians drop the ingredient being tested into rabbits' eyes, rub it on the skin of rats, which are then blood tested and examined for organ damage, and inject it into mice to test for cancer. At the first danger signal, the ingredient is rejected. Although cosmetics testing is voluntary and —amazingly—not required by law in the United States, and although the research budget amounts to only $\frac{1}{2}$ to 1 percent of the total operating budget (compared to about 10 percent in the drug industry), many feel the testing is adequate and the dangers minimal.

Even so, the United States is still in the dark ages of cosmetics control compared to other nations of the world.

Many countries have much tighter laws governing the manufacture and sale of cosmetics. Spain requires the pretesting that is voluntary here; Japan licenses manufacturers (the United States now requires them to register); Switzerland controls certain products, such as vaginal deodorants, as drugs rather than cosmetics; France won't allow certain terms with medical definitions—such as allergy and dandruff—to be used in advertising. A number of ingredients strictly banned elsewhere, such as certain chemicals in hair dyes and vitamins in face creams, are still permitted in American cosmetics. We've made progress, but we still have a long way to go.

LAST RESORT: SURGERY

When hope is not enough, when cosmetics can do no more to fulfill the ideal of beauty, the plastic surgeon takes over. An outgrowth of surgical techniques developed to restore the faces of men disfigured by war wounds, plastic surgery has been part of the Hollywood scene for a long time. Marilyn Monroe, a film star of the 1950's famous for her beautiful body, had plastic surgery—on her *chin*. It had been rather weak looking; after it was firmed up by a chin implant, stardom was within reach. Singer Barbra Streisand, on the other hand, refused to have the "nose job" that was generally expected of an aspiring star; she felt her aquiline nose gave her a distinctive look and would not change it.

The French writer and artist Jean Cocteau once wrote, "A defect of the soul cannot be corrected on the face—but a defect of the face, if you *can* correct it, can correct a soul." For most people, surgery is unnecessary, and their individual differences simply don't bother them. But for some, having a nose that is much too large or misshapen can be a real psychological problem, and for them plastic surgery is a good solution. Not all surgeons are as optimistic as Cocteau about the benefits of correcting the defect, warning that patients who expect the operation to change a whole life are in for a disappointment.

Cosmetic surgery can make small breasts larger. And in a society where big breasts (but not too big) are nearly as essential as small noses, many young women, especially hopeful actresses, have this surgery performed. The size of a woman's breasts is determined by heredity and by her general weight, as well as by hormonal changes such as those of pregnancy and nursing a child. Breasts can't be made larger by the use of any creams or gadgets, no matter what the ads claim. Exercise doesn't increase the size of breasts either, but it can improve the tone of the muscles that support them, making them *look* bigger. For people with the opposite problem, surgery can make large breasts smaller.

Probably the most popular kind of plastic surgery is the face lift, in which the sagging skin of an aging person is tightened by removing some skin around the hairline where the hair will conceal the scars. The surgery is expensive, the recovery time is several weeks, some say the lifted face looks masklike, and the lift doesn't last long—only until additional aging again takes its toll—but the result is usually good, and many wealthy women would not want to face another birthday without it.

Some beauty experts recommend regular exercise of the facial muscles—there are fifty-five of them—to delay the onslaught of sagging skin. But experts on the other side of the controversy deride the idea, claiming that even if a woman were able to do such exercises twenty-four hours a day, seven days a week, she could not keep pace with the natural erosion of age. What's more, overdoing the exercises might even *produce* wrinkles.

MEN PAINTING

For a variety of reasons that have to do with our society's attitudes toward youth, beauty, and the status of women, the gray hairs and wrinkles that make a woman feel old and unattractive somehow seem to make a man appear mature and distinguished. But throughout history men, too, have used cosmetics. At times they have painted and powdered their faces even more than women have.

Englishmen in the court of Queen Elizabeth I wore a great deal of makeup. They worried about their complexions and sometimes even wore masks to protect their skin from the sun. They dyed their hair auburn and grew a single long lock, which they tied over one shoulder with a pretty ribbon. They lavished perfume on themselves, dressed up in all sorts of fancy hats, clothes, and ruffs, and carried perfumed gloves.

In eighteenth-century England the Macaroni decked himself out in extreme styles brought from Italy and carried men's fashions and cosmetics to a new extreme. (The American Revolutionary War song, "Yankee Doodle Dandy," refers to the Macaronis and their dandified dress.) Although there was a reaction against this extreme, some men were still rouging their cheeks in the nineteenth century.

Once again, after several generations of rejection, cosmetics are tempting men. But selling cosmetics to men is still not easy. They traditionally think of themselves as existing beyond the need to beautify themselves, although they have often urged beautification on women (as long as they couldn't detect anything artificial about it). That rugged image is gradually being worn down. After World War II, any perfumed preparation that had the word *shave* in it was all right. Eventually men's colognes gained favor, given tough masculine names and packaging that seems muscular and woodsy.

Men have begun to dye and curl their hair; many are using fast-tanning products for a bronze appearance suggesting a vigorous outdoor life. People who predict such things say it may not be long before men begin to shape and darken their eyebrows as well, and they may experiment with lipstick. But the shades of men's cosmetics will probably range in the browns and tans; the day of bright-colored makeup for men is not yet in sight.

LOOKING AHEAD

The continued use of cosmetics seems certain. It's unlikely that we will ever return to the stern prohibition against makeup that marked certain eras, mostly because the cosmetics industry has too much at stake and is too powerful to let that happen. Instead, the cycle will run between the obviously painted look and the natural look that requires just as many different products and just as much skill so you don't appear to be painted when you actually are.

Perhaps there will at some time in the future be ways to eliminate acne and to prevent aging; people will have naturally smooth, healthy skins through their long lives. As life-spans continue to lengthen so that in another generation or so people may look forward to living a century or more, they will be more determined than ever to look young longer.

Product safety will continue to be questioned, just as it is in the drug industry; as long as new products are being tried out, safety is a concern, no matter how thorough the testing. Among the things that may come up for testing in the future: pills to prevent sunburn, to eliminate body odor, to change hair color.

Cosmetics have been a way of identifying certain groups of people. Women in Eastern cities don't follow quite the same makeup or hair styles endorsed by women in small towns in the South or rural areas of the Midwest; the society lady makes up differently from the secretary or factory worker; young girls don't make up like their mothers. In the future, then, cosmetics could be used in two ways: to help people look more alike, or to help define individual differences. But one thing is certain: they will never be eliminated. We've needed them since earliest times for our pursuit of the unattainable goal of perfect beauty. Even when we fall short of the ideal, cosmetics help us to enjoy the fullest possible measure of attractiveness, love, and good feelings about ourselves.

BIBLIOGRAPHY

Angeloglou, Maggie. *A History of Make-Up.* New York: The Macmillan Co., 1970.

Corson, Richard. *Fashions in Makeup.* New York: Universe Books, Inc., 1972.

Donnan, Marcia. *Cosmetics from the Kitchen.* New York: Holt, Rinehart & Winston, 1972.

Harry, Ralph G. *Modern Cosmeticology*, 3rd rev. ed. Brooklyn: Chemical Publishing Co., Inc., 1947.

Hauser, Gayelord. *Mirror, Mirror on the Wall: Invitation to Beauty.* New York: Farrar, Straus & Cudahy, 1961.

Lawson, Donna. *Mother Nature's Beauty Cupboard.* New York: Thomas Y. Crowell, Co., 1973.

Miller, Melba. *The Black Is Beautiful Beauty Book.* Englewood Cliffs: Prentice-Hall, Inc., 1974.

Perutz, Kathrin. *Beyond the Looking Glass.* New York: William Morrow & Co., 1970.

Plummer, Beverly. *Fragrance: How to Make Natural Soaps, Scents and Sundries.* New York: Atheneum Publishers, 1975.

Rutledge, Deborah. *Natural Beauty Secrets.* New York: Hawthorn Books, Inc., 1966.

Shelmire, Bedford, Jr. *The Art of Being Beautiful at Any Age.* New York: St. Martins Press, Inc., 1975.

Stabile, Toni. *Cosmetics: Trick or Treat?* New York: Hawthorn Books, Inc., 1966.

Tobias, Andrew. *Fire and Ice: The Story of Charles Revson—the Man Who Built the Revlon Empire.* New York: William Morrow & Co., 1976.

Verrill, A. Hyatt. *Perfumes and Spices.* Boston: L. C. Page & Co., 1940.

Winter, Ruth. *A Consumer's Dictionary of Cosmetic Ingredients.* New York: Crown Publishers, Inc., 1974.

INDEX

Acid mantle, 20, 26
Advertising, 13-14, 23, 27, 29, 32, 68, 70, 74-76, 79-81, 88
Aging, 15-17, 29, 43-44, 54, 88, 91
Alcohol, 28, 39-41
Allergies, 23, 25, 55, 78, 82-84, 86
Antiperspirants, 37
Antiseptics, 37, 61
Arden, Elizabeth, 71
Astringents, 26-28
Avocado, 26, 75
Avon, 71, 74
Ayer, Harriet Hubbard, 68-69
Bacteria, 20, 28, 36-37, 83
Baking soda, 36, 44, 61
Baldness, 50, 56-57
Banana, 26
Baths, 28, 30-31, 33-37, 85; baking soda, 36; salts, 34
Beauty, 71, 75, 81, 89-90, 92; definition of, 9-14, 47; salons, 13, 56
Benzoin, tincture of, 77-78
Blonde rinse, 49-50
Bosom and breasts, 27, 66, 88
Brunette rinse, 50
Butter, 46, 50; cocoa, 44, 46; -milk, 27-28, 44
Cancer, 29, 43, 85

Casein, 78
Citric Acid, 78
Cleopatra, 25, 58, 65, 74
Cologne, 39, 71, 90
Consumers, 76-78
Cornmeal, 45
Cornstarch, 37-38, 82
Cosmetics, 12; definition, 14; history, 13-14, 65-67, 71-76, 89-90; homemade, 67, 78; hypo-allergenic, 78, 83; industry, 11, 13-15, 23, 29, 68-84, 91; ingredients, 23-25, 33, 75-86; makeup, 65-68, 70-74, 81, 83-84, 89, 91-92; men's, 89-91; natural, 25, 55, 75
Creams, 19, 21, 24-25, 28-29, 68-70, 75, 78, 86
Cucumber, 24-25, 34, 75
Dandruff, 51, 86
Deodorants, 37, 85
Depilatories, 58-59
Detergents, 32-33, 44, 48-49
Diet, 18, 24, 75
Egg-white mask, 21
Electrolysis, 59
Elizabeth I, 66, 89
Emollients, 22-26, 29, 41, 44, 46, 67, 84
Enfleurage, 40-41

Exercise, 18, 88
Eye(s), 47, 56, 61-62, 65-66, 84; -brows, 10-11, 56, 66, 91; drops, 62; -lashes, 56, 82; makeup, 65, 70-71, 74, 83-84; -wash, boric acid, 62
Factor, Max, 71, 74
Fats and oils, 46; greases, 31-32, 39, 44, 50
Feet, 34, 36, 46
Feminine hygiene sprays, 85
Films, 11, 73-74, 86-87
Fingernails, 44, 46, 55, 84
Flowers, 35, 38-41
Food and Drug Administration, 77, 85
Food, Drug and Cosmetic Act, 14, 82, 84
Freckles, 42
Fuller's earth mask, 21-22
Glands, apocrine, 36; eccrine, 36; sebaceous, 15-16, 28, 48; sweat, 15-16, 36
Glycerin, and cucumber, 34; and lemon juice, 45; and rosewater, 45
Hair, 11, 47-59; bleaching, 47, 54, 56, 59; body, 58-59; brushing, 51-52; cells, 48, 54-55; conditioning, 50-51, 78; curling, 47, 52, 54, 58, 90; -dressers, 48, 58; dryness, 51; dyeing, 47-48, 54-57, 74-75, 80, 86, 89-90, 92; facial, 59; follicles, 15, 48, 54, 59; gray, 47, 54-55, 80, 89; removers, 58-59; rinses, 48-52, 56; sprays, 54, 75; straightening, 47, 53-54; washing, 48-49, 51, 78
Hands, 36, 44-46
Health, 10, 15, 17, 46, 67-68, 71, 91
Henna, 55
Herb(s), 35, 40, 70; -and-flower bath, 35
Heredity, 15, 17, 48, 54, 57, 88
Honey, 26
Hormones, 16, 29, 88
Humectants, 24, 78
Infusion, 40
Kohl, 65, 74
Labeling, 77-78, 82
Lanolin, 23
Lard, 23, 40-41, 44
Laws, 56, 66-67, 76-78, 81-82, 84-86
Lead poisoning, 66, 81
Lecithin, 77
Lemon juice, 20, 26, 42, 45, 49, 62
Lip makeup, 67, 70-74, 78-79, 91
Lotions, 25-26, 45, 48, 55, 70, 78
Maceration, 40
Makeup, see Cosmetics
Masks, 21-22, 89
Mayonnaise, 26, 51

Melanin, 42
Milk, 28, 33, 78
Moisturizers, *see* Emollients
Mouthwash, 60-61
Nail polish, 72, 84
Oatmeal, 20, 26, 34-35, 45; scrubber, 20
Odors, 36-37, 45, 83, 85, 92
Oil, 23-24, 26, 29-31, 44-46, 49, 51; essential, 39, 41-42; mineral, 24, 28, 40, 84; olive, 28, 31, 46, 51
Packaging, 14, 27, 29, 78-79
Pancake, *see* Cosmetics, makeup
Parsley, 61
Patch test, 55-56
Perfume, 37-42, 67, 78, 82-83, 89-90
Permanent wave, 52, 55, 59
Petroleum jelly, 24, 70
Pigment, 42, 54-56, 78
Pomade, 41, 53
Potato, 45
Powder, body, 37-38; face, 66, 70, 72, 74, 81, 84
Product Safety, 75-76, 84, 91-92; testing, 82, 85, 92
Propylene Glycol, 78
Protein, 46, 50, 78
Pumice stone, 46, 60-61
Revlon, 71, 74, 78-80
Rosewater, 45
Rouge, 71-72, 89
Rubinstein, Helena, 69-71

Salt, 34, 46, 61
Scalp, 48, 51
Sebum, 15-16, 20
Shaving, 58-59
Skin, 10, 14-18, 20-24, 25-29, 33-36, 42-46, 48, 50; cells, 15, 18, 21, 34; dermis, 15, 36; epidermis, 15-16, 18; foods, 24-26; pores, 16, 18, 20-21, 26, 70; problems, 15-17, 18, 21, 22-23, 24, 26, 28, 29, 32, 34, 43, 44, 70, 88, 91
Soap, 19-21, 24, 31-32, 45, 48-49, 82, 85
Strawberries, 25-26, 33, 75, 84
Sunburn, 22, 42-44, 92
Suntan, 10, 42-44, 72, 90
Surgery, plastic, 12, 86-88
Sweat, 36-37
Tannic acid, 28, 61, 62
Tea-bag treatment, 62
Teeth, 47, 60-61, 67
Tomato, 26, 44, 75
Toothpaste, 60-61; powder, 61
Vinegar, 44, 49, 51, 55; cosmetic, 20
Vitamins, 18, 28, 30, 42, 86
Water, 19-21, 23, 28-36, 40, 44-46, 49, 77, 85
Wigs, 48, 56-58, 66-67
Witch hazel, 28, 37
World War I, 71; II, 72-73, 90
Yogurt, 28, 44

96